★ ★ ★ ★ ★ ★ ★ ★ ★ ★ ★ ★ ★ ★ ★ ★ ★ ★

WOMEN OF AMERICA

Clara Barton

RED CROSS PIONEER

MATTHEW G. GRANT

Illustrated by John Keely

GALLERY OF GREAT AMERICANS SERIES

★ ★

Clara Barton

RED CROSS PIONEER

Text copyright © 1974 by Publication Associates. Illustrations copyright © 1974 by Creative Education. International copyrights reserved in all countries. No part of this book may be reproduced in any form without written permission from the publisher. Printed in the United States.

Library of Congress Number: 73-15869   ISBN: 0-87191-306-2

Published by Creative Education, Mankato, Minnesota 56001
Distributed by Childrens Press, 1224 West Van Buren Street, Chicago, Illinois 60607

LIBRARY OF CONGRESS CATALOGING IN PUBLICATION DATA
Grant, Matthew G.
    Clara Barton—Red Cross pioneer.
    (His Gallery of great Americans series. Women of America)
    SUMMARY: A biography of the teacher, nurse, and founder of the American Red Cross.
    1. Barton, Clara Harlowe, 1821-1912 — Juvenile literature. [1. Barton, Clara Harlow, 1821-1912. 2. Nurses and nursing. 3. Red Cross. United States. American National Red Cross] I. Keely, John, illus. II. Title.
HV569.B3G73   361.7'7 [B] [92]   73-15869
ISBN 0-87191-306-2

1. Geneva, Switzerland. discusses foundation of Red Cross
2. Strasbourg, France. aids civilian victims of Franco-Prussian War

CONTENTS

SCENES OF CLARA BARTON'S LIFE

1. born North Oxford, Mass.
2. 1852, Bordentown, N.J. Sets up first public school in N.J.
3. 1854-61, Washington, D.C. one of first women government employees
4. Culpepper, Va. first nurses wounded at *Battle of Cedar Mtn*
   nurses at: Second Battle of Bull Run   Battle of Chantilly
        Antietam   Frederickburg   Charleston, S.C. battles
5. sets up national cemetery at Andersonville, Ga.
6. establishes first local Red Cross unit, Danville, N.Y.
7. Glen Echo, Md. last home and place of death

THE GIRL NURSE

Clarissa Barton was 11 years old when her brother, David, fell off the barn. Doctors said David would probably die. But the little girl said: ''I will take care of him.''

For two years she tended him. In 1834, David finally got well. The doctor said: ''Clara

is a natural nurse. She had saved her brother's life."

Everyone called her Clara. She was the youngest in the family, a tiny girl who loved to ride horseback. She would listen wide-eyed to her father's tales of the Indian Wars. Sometimes she wept as he told how the wounded soldiers suffered.

Both her sisters and her eldest brother were teachers. When Clara was 18, she became a teacher, too. Her shyness melted away as she coped with rowdy boys. She became a great organizer, beloved for her sense of humor.

Clara taught school for 15 years. Several men wanted to marry her, but she told them she did not love them. She preferred to be independent.

In 1854, when she was 33, she was exhausted from teaching. She went to work as a clerk in the Patent Office in Washington—one of the first women to work in government. It was an interesting job and she made many friends among the politicians.

Then, in 1861, the Civil War broke out. Troops from Clara's home state of Massachusetts came to Washington—and they needed help.

The soldiers had been attacked by a mob. Their baggage had been stolen. Clara got her friends to provide clothes and other supplies for the men. She helped the soldiers write letters to their families.

Battles raged around Washington. Clara heard how wounded men were suffering on the battlefields and she determined to help them. First, she wrote to her friends, asking for money for medical supplies.

ANGEL OF THE BATTLEFIELD

Clara Barton then went to Union Army officials and asked to be allowed to go to the battlefield in Virginia. Red tape was sliced freely to allow the determined little woman to carry out her plan.

Clara took a mule team loaded with medical supplies. She arrived at Culpeper,

Virginia, two days after the Battle of Cedar Mountain. Wounded men lay everywhere. The army hospital was out of dressings. Clara and her supplies seemed like a miracle to the hard-working army doctors. She herself went to help the men still lying on the field. She fed them and gave them water. She brought warm clothes and comforted the dying.

Dr. James Dunn, the brigade surgeon, said: "She was like an angel. An angel of the battlefield."

Clara knew that the wounded would receive good care once they reached army hospitals. But her concern was for the men at the front. Many were dying of thirst and loss of blood before they could be safely evacuated. These were the men Clara set out to help. She did this work all through the war.

THE AMERICAN RED CROSS

When the Civil War ended, Clara Barton was famous. Almost single-handedly, she had changed the method of dealing with the wounded on the battlefield. She was treated as a heroine.

For some time, Clara devoted herself to the sad but necessary work of identifying unknown Union dead. She helped to set up a National Cemetery at Andersonville, Georgia, site of a large prison camp.

After this, Clara became a lecturer. She told eager listeners about her war work. She also became a champion of women's rights and a friend of Susan B. Anthony, Lucy Stone, and other pioneer feminists.

By 1869, Clara was once more very tired. She went on a vacation to Europe in order to regain her strength.

In Geneva, Switzerland, Dr. Louis Appia

told her about the work of the Red Cross. It

was an international group devoted to caring

for the wounded in wartime. Clara became

keenly interested. At that time the Franco-

Prussian War broke out and Clara went to

observe the Red Cross in action.

Clara helped the suffering civilians of Strasbourg, whose city had been pounded by a siege. She saw that the Red Cross workers helped victims of war no matter what their nationality. She resolved to do her best to introduce the Red Cross into the United States.

But once more Clara's health broke down. It was several years before she returned home. Not until 1877 was she able to return to work.

When she was well again, she began
urging Congress and the President to join the
other nations of the world in the Red Cross.
But at first she had no luck. People in government were sure that America would never
again go to war. What need was there for

the Red Cross? Clara pointed out that the Red Cross could be of service during natural disasters, too. She was the first to suggest this kind of Red Cross work.

In 1881 Clara set up the first local Red Cross unit in Dansville, N.Y. That very year there was a huge forest fire in Michigan. Red Cross units from Dansville, Rochester, and Syracuse sent help.

Newspapers wrote about the work of mercy. Other cities set up Red Cross units. Finally, on March 1, 1882, President Chester Arthur signed the Treaty of Geneva and the American Red Cross was born.

ONCE MORE INTO BATTLE

Clara Barton became the first president of the American Red Cross. She was an old woman but full of new energy. She helped organize Red Cross units all over the United States.

During the following years the Red Cross and Clara Barton aided the victims of floods,

tornadoes, earthquakes, and disease epidem-
ics. Red Cross workers not only nursed the
sick and injured but also provided money to
rebuild homes and replant lost crops.

The American Red Cross also helped to
feed starving people in Russia and Armenia.
In 1898 Clara took food to Cuba, where a
revolution was raging.

The U.S. battleship Maine was blown
up in Havana harbor. The Spanish-American
War began. Once more Clara found herself
aiding wounded Americans on the battlefield.
She was 77 years old. When the war ended,
Congress voted her the nation's thanks.

Clara Barton retired from the Red Cross
in 1904. Not willing to be idle, she set up
the National First Aid Association.

The rest of her days were spent in writing books about the Red Cross and her childhood, and letters to her many friends around the world. She still made an occasional speech and also found time to garden, repair furniture, and learn to typewrite.

Clara Barton died April 12, 1912, at the age of 91. She was buried at her birthplace, North Oxford. The Red Cross flag is her monument.

★ ★

GALLERY OF GREAT AMERICANS SERIES

★ ★

INDIANS OF AMERICA
- GERONIMO
- CRAZY HORSE
- CHIEF JOSEPH
- PONTIAC
- SQUANTO
- OSCEOLA

EXPLORERS OF AMERICA
- COLUMBUS
- LEIF ERICSON
- DeSOTO
- LEWIS AND CLARK
- CHAMPLAIN
- CORONADO

FRONTIERSMEN OF AMERICA
- DANIEL BOONE
- BUFFALO BILL
- JIM BRIDGER
- FRANCIS MARION
- DAVY CROCKETT
- KIT CARSON

WAR HEROES OF AMERICA
- JOHN PAUL JONES
- PAUL REVERE
- ROBERT E. LEE
- ULYSSES S. GRANT
- SAM HOUSTON
- LAFAYETTE

WOMEN OF AMERICA
- CLARA BARTON
- JANE ADDAMS
- ELIZABETH BLACKWELL
- HARRIET TUBMAN
- SUSAN B. ANTHONY
- DOLLEY MADISON

★ ★

12,076

B
02
BAR

Grant, Matthew
G.
Clara Barton,
Red Cross pioneer.

Date Due	Borrower's Name	Room No.
FEB 14 1977	Andys Fetter	502
DE 23 77	Ber nadette	13
JE 9 78	anice Gordan	503
AP 9 '81	Ethel Hlerum	

B
02
BAR

Grant, Matthew
G.
Clara Barton,
Red Cross pioneer.

12076